THE ENRON/ ARTHUR ANDERSEN DEBACLE

THE ENRON/ ARTHUR ANDERSEN DEBACLE:
A Case Study and Legal Implications

Michael B. Bixby
Boise State University

Pearson Education

Upper Saddle River, New Jersey 07458

Acquisitions editor: David Parker
Assistant editor: Ashley Keim
Production editor: Carol Zaino
Manufacturer: Courier (Bookmart Press, Inc.)

Copyright ©2003 by Prentice-Hall, Inc., Upper Saddle River, New Jersey, 07458. All rights reserved. Printed in the United States of America. This publication is protected by copyright, and permission should be obtained from the publisher prior to any prohibited reproduction, storage in a retrieval system, or transmission in any form or by any means, electronic, mechanical, photocopying, recording, or likewise. For information regarding permission(s), write to: Rights and Permissions Department.

ISBN 0-13-146097-8

10 9 8 7 6

THE ENRON/ARTHUR ANDERSEN DEBACLE:
A Case Study and Legal Implications

By Michael B. Bixby
Professor, Legal Studies in Business
Boise State University

Introduction

In early 2001 Enron Corporation was listed #5 on the list of "Fortune 500" corporations (just behind Ford Motor Company and ahead of General Electric) based on its revenue. In a little over 15 years Enron had grown from a modest Houston gas pipeline company into a $100 billion-a-year business. Its stock was selling in excess of $80 per share, giving the company a total equity of some $60 billion. Enron owned power companies and pipelines around the world, and had pioneered the energy trading business. Meanwhile its auditor, Arthur Andersen LLP (limited liability partnership), was one of the most venerable and respected of the "Big 5" international auditing and accounting firms, with a robust consulting practice as well.

However, by early 2002, the "Enron Debacle" had left the company itself in Chapter 11 bankruptcy, thousands of Enron employees had been laid off, and many also lost their retirement savings which were mostly invested in Enron stock. T thousands of Enron shareholders have been left holding now-worthless Enron stock, while its former executives have become notorious public figures due to their questionable financial and management actions. The corporation and its executives are facing dozens of lawsuits by angry investors and creditors. At least ten Congressional committees and several government agencies, including a Justice Department criminal task force, are looking into Enron. Meanwhile, after a month-long trial, Arthur Andersen LLP has been found guilty of federal criminal charges of "obstruction of justice," and is facing numerous civil lawsuits for malpractice due to its assistance in the preparation of, and certification of misleading Enron financial reports. The firm itself is not likely to be in existence much longer. Both Enron and Andersen—considered among the very top firms in their respective fields about one year ago—have for much of 2002 been prominently featured (in a negative sense) on the nightly news shows and have become the subject of jokes by comedians and talk show hosts. What are the events that caused such a fall? How has all this happened in only one year? What are some of the legal implications? This case study will explore the events which led to the downfall of these two prominent firms, in an attempt to recognize the mistakes which were made and the lessons to be learned.

While the events of the last year have had catastrophic effects upon Enron and its employees, officers, creditors and investors, as well as the partners, employees and clients of Arthur Andersen, the fallout from the Enron debacle has had a much wider impact. As the result of the Enron scandal, many corporations, investors, auditors, analysts, financial experts, Congress, government regulators and the media have looked more closely at corporate financial statements, and in case after case, such records have proved to be inaccurate and misleading.

The stunning disclosure in late June 2002 that WorldCom Inc. had improperly accounted for $3.8 billion of charges paid to local telephone networks to complete calls as capital expenditures rather than expenses (which made profits seem much larger than they really were), has caused a profound loss of trust by investors, financial institutions and the general public in the accuracy of corporate accounting and financial records. Public confidence in large corporations, their executives and financial officers has reached an all-time low. A poll conducted even before the WorldCom disclosures showed that 57% of Americans said they do not trust corporate executives or brokerage firms to give them honest information, and the number is probably higher now. (*Americans Distrust Institutions in Poll*, Wall St. Journal, June 13, 2002) It is likely that major changes in the way companies are governed and regulated, and the manner in which their financial records are maintained and disclosed, will result from these disclosures. Since the rise and fall of Enron, coupled with the role of its auditor Arthur Andersen, led to all of the further investigations, it is instructive to take a close look at the Enron/Andersen chain of events.

Enron Corporation

Founding and Growth of the Company

In July 1985, two gas pipeline companies--InterNorth Corp. and Houston Natural Gas Co. merged, creating a 37,000-mile pipeline network, the nation's biggest coast-to-coast system. By February 1986, the chairman of Houston Natural Gas, Mr. Kenneth Lay, had taken over as CEO of the combined company and the firm name was changed to Enron. Mr. Lay, after a poor childhood, had obtained undergraduate and masters degrees from the University of Missouri, then worked as an economist for Humble Oil Co. and served in the U.S. Navy. He married and moved to Washington, DC in 1971 for several years, first working as speechwriter and aide with his former professor at the Federal Power Commission (which is now the Federal Energy Regulatory Commission) then serving as Deputy undersecretary at the Department of Energy. During this time Mr. Lay became a vigorous crusader for and advocate of energy deregulation. While working in Washington, he continued to work on, and did complete, a PhD. in economics from the University of Houston. Mr. Lay left Washington in 1974 for private industry, and spent the next 11 years moving up into increasingly more important positions within the natural gas industry, first in Florida and then in Texas. After ten years of Mr. Lay's leadership Enron grew to become the largest combined gas and electricity company in the United States by 1996, with assets of $16 billion and revenue of $13 billion.

Enron Begins to Change

In 1989 Enron began the trading of natural gas commodities, and in 1994 it began to trade units of electricity. Essentially this means that Enron would enter into contracts to purchase from one source, and to supply to another company or utility, units of electricity or natural gas (so many cubic feet, for example) during a particular time period in the future. Although market prices fluctuated, Enron hoped to, and often did, earn a profit on the transactions. Enron eventually entered into thousands of such contracts. The loosening of government controls on the natural gas business in the 1980s (with Mr. Lay as one of the leading proponents) led to the deregulation of electricity in the 1990s, which really created the energy-trading industry. Enron quickly and steadily moved into the forefront of this new business, aggressively buying and selling electricity contracts, natural gas pipelines, wastewater management and power plants, to wholesale suppliers and retail customers worldwide.

By the late 1990s Enron's reported profits came mostly from marketing and trading in energy contracts—meaning the company guaranteed a specific price at which a certain amount of gas, oil or electricity could be supplied sometime in the future. Enron became a darling of Wall Street due to its massive growth in revenues and stated profits, with the company often delivering shareholders a 200 percent return on their investments. By 2000, the company had expanded its operations beyond the traditional energy business, moving into ventures like online trading of energy and telecommunication commodities (largely through its internet vehicle, Enron OnLine), providing risk-management consulting services and trading Internet broadband services (the right to certain units of high-speed internet access). Indeed some 80% of its earning came from a vague business known as "wholesale energy operations and services." At its peak the company employed nearly 21,000 people worldwide, and had projects in India, South America and Europe. Enron was a hot company, ahead of the curve in many areas, and hiring the "best and brightest." People rallied behind Mr. Lay and his new ideas for the energy business. Analysts, brokers, traders and others were making a lot of money, and people liked Ken Lay. He remembered names, and jotted personal notes on memos. He liked jawing with pipeline operators and fellow PhD's alike.

For six consecutive years Enron was voted Most Innovative among Fortune's Most Admired Companies. After moving aggressively into trading of all types of commodities, Enron's revenues shot from $31 billion in 1998 to more than $100 billion in 2000. With legions of traders working out of its Houston skyscraper, the company put together a business structure so complex it mystified many Wall Street veterans. Not content to be the largest energy trading company, Enron aimed higher. In early 2001, a banner was hung in the Enron lobby proclaiming it "The World's Leading Company."

The Roles of Kenneth Lay and Jeffrey Skilling

As Enron grew, so did Kenneth Lay's involvement in politics, civic projects, and charity work. Mr. Lay had become friends with Texas governor George W. Bush, and at his request served as co-chairman of the 1990 economic summit in Houston. Two years later Mr. Lay was named chairman of the host committee for the GOP convention. He became one of the largest contributors to Mr. Bush's presidential campaign, and celebrated his election as president of the United States with Mr. and Mrs. Bush and other Republican and business leaders. According to several reports, President Bush called Mr. Lay by the nickname "Kenny Boy." Mr. Lay and his wife also contributed and raised millions of dollars for the Houston United Way, the local Holocaust Museum, the United Negro College fund, and other charities. He embraced his role as "Mr. Outside," the company's statesman and chief lobbyist, gave many speeches, was active in local and national affairs, and he became well-known to important people across the country. While still CEO of Enron during the mid-1990s, Mr. Lay began to turn more of the day-to-day management to others. For several years, Richard Kinder, a Missouri classmate of Mr. Lay's served at president and chief operating officer (COO). After Mr. Kinder left Enron at the end of 1996, Jeffrey Skilling, formerly the chief finance officer, became president and COO. Mr. Skilling, a brilliant, aggressive, and cocky former McKinsey & Co. consultant and Harvard MBA, had been hired by Mr. Lay in 1990 to head and build the Enron Capital & Trade energy trading unit.

In retrospect, many have commented that Enron leadership, starting with Mr. Skilling, epitomized the word "arrogance." The company came to believe that older stodgier competitors had no chance against the sleek, modern Enron juggernaut. "These big companies (like ExxonMobil) will topple over from their own weight," Mr. Skilling said at a conference a year or so ago, at which he also insisted that Enron's then share price of about $80/share really should be closer to $126/share

Enron complicated matters by refusing to clarify much about its financial details. According to a reporter for Fortune Magazine, the leaders of the company thought they were smarter than anyone else, and as long as the money continued to roll in, were not forthcoming with many details. When the Fortune reporter asked questions about Enron's nearly incomprehensible financial statements, Mr. Skilling replied, "Our business is not a black box. It's very simple to model. People who raise questions are people who have not gone through it in detail. We have explicit answers, but people want to throw rocks at us." (*Fortune*, Dec. 24, 2001) "Perhaps the biggest culprit was arrogance, which caused Enron to be compared to past self-proclaimed masters of the universe such as Drexel Burnham Lambert in the 1980s and Long-Term Capital Management in the 1990s." (Business Week, Dec. 10, 2001)

Mr. Lay stepped down as CEO in February 2001, and installed Mr. Skilling in the post. Mr. Skilling thought there were two kinds of people in the world—those who "got it" and those who didn't. "It" was Enron's complex strategy of making rich profits and returns from a trading and risk-management business built on assets owned by others. Vertically integrated behemoths like ExxonMobil who owned oil reserves, gas stations, and other assets, were dinosaurs to a contemptuous Skilling. "In the old days, people worked for the assets, he stated, but "we've turned it around—now the assets work for people." One former executive stated that "Jeff's theory was that assets were bad, and intellectual capital was good." But neither the shareholders, board members, employees, bankers, auditors, nor financial analysts fully understood how Enron was funded, and the incredible levels of debt Enron had taken on. Everyone was willing to go along, as long as Enron had ever-increasing earnings and revenue. Accounting rules allowed Enron to count all its contracts for energy trading (not just the profits) as "revenue." That technique caused Enron's revenues to dramatically increase, even though the company was not actually generating or producing additional energy. This high revenue level helped to boost Enron's stock price, and kept its credit rating high, thus allowing it to borrow enormous amounts at good rates. [Enron's bankruptcy filings later showed $13.1 billion in debt for Enron, and an additional $18 billion for Enron affiliates. That doesn't include however, an estimated $20 billion additional debt in the off-balance sheets entities.](*Business Week,* Dec. 10, 2001)

However during the first half of 2001 Enron's share price fell steadily, to about $40--half of its former level--by August. The firm had been criticized following the summer of 2000 when following deregulation an energy crisis in California caused power shortages, brownouts, huge increases in energy costs to consumers and the bankruptcy of California's largest electrical utility. Enron, through its numerous contracts for purchases and sales of electricity, was directly involved, and some alleged that Enron and other energy traders' actions were part of the reason for the steep increases in cost. There were allegations that manipulation of power and prices had occurred.

Enron also was losing money on some of its investments in foreign ventures involving electrical and water projects, and in such unusual activities as bandwidth trading. A large part of Mr. Skilling's emphasis at Enron had been to promote the use of supercomputers and fiber-optic cable to turn the former natural gas and energy business into a worldwide trading firm. As Peter Fusar, president of Gobal Change Associates, a consulting firm that has studied Enron says, "They tried to commoditize everything." (i.e. to trade units of electricity, natural gas, telecommunications time, rather than to produce a product) The ultimate goal was never to touch another cubic foot of natural gas, yet to make billions by trading it.

Mr. Skilling boldly proclaimed that Enron would rocket past ExxonMobil to become the world's leading energy firm—quite an ambition since Exxon had announced a $4 billion profit—but Mr. Skilling had even higher goals. He believed he had a business insight so powerful that it would transform Enron into the world's leading company, period. His vision was that deregulation and market forces would force traditional, asset-heavy companies to break up into thousands of niche players. Skilling wanted Enron to be "asset-light." Rather than being vertically integrated, companies would be "virtually integrated"—by enterprises such as Enron that would "wire those thousands of firms back together cheaply and temporarily." (*Economist*, Dec. 8, 2001)

Because Enron operated in a largely unregulated arena and because of the way energy trading firms are allowed to account for their operations, the company recorded revenue that made the economic status of the business appear larger than it really was. Under accounting rules, when an energy trading company trades electricity or gas, it can count as revenues the whole amount of every transaction rather than simply the profit or loss, as a brokerage firm does. That is how Enron, a relative newcomer to the trading of commodities and related financial instruments, was able to produce $101 billion of revenue in 2000, up from $40 billion in 1999. (New York Times, Jan. 14, 2002)

The Decline Begins

But Mr. Skilling made a big mistake. Enron, already saddled with about $5 billion in money-losing investments from utility projects around the world, had borrowed another $1 billion to increase its capacity to trade datatransmission on fiber-optic cable.

Enron insiders say that to minimize the impact of this debt on Enron's financial statements, Skilling and Enron's Chief Finance Officer Andrew Fastow began to create complicated off-balance-sheet private partnerships that did business with Enron but whose finances were not subject to much scrutiny at Enron. Considerable Enron debt was transferred to these partnerships and thus off the books of Enron. CFO Fastow acted as general manger of several of the "off-book" partnerships (also called Special Purpose Entities or SPEs), and received huge personal financial benefits as well. Reports indicate that he personally received as much as $30 million for his services to these entities. The potential for conflict of interest and violation of fiduciary duty seemed overwhelming. "Internally, everybody said this is not a good idea," a source close to the company told *Business Week*. (Nov. 12, 2001)

Then in August 2001 (after less than six months as CEO), Mr. Skilling shocked the energy and financial community by abruptly resigning from his post, without an explanation other than "personal reasons." Mr. Skilling didn't like to explain much anyway—during his tenure as CEO he had once called an analyst an "ass____" when the analyst asked Skilling to produce Enron's balance sheet during a conference call. (*The Enron Debacle*, Business Week, Nov. 12, 2001) Kenneth Lay, the chairman, once again assumed the CEO position of the company he had founded 15 years earlier. Mr. Lay, who had left most day-to-day management to Mr. Skilling since 1997, was never able to clearly explain how the partnerships worked or why anyone should not assume the worst—that they were set up to hide Enron's problems, inflate earnings, and personally benefit the executives who managed them.

What only became clear after Enron's fall was that the company's spectacular success was built on fraudulent and misleading financial reporting and "aggressive" accounting practices (some call it "cooking the books") designed solely to increase the share price. In fact, the company's 2000 annual report states that Enron is "laser-focused on earnings per share (EPS) and we expect to continue strong earnings performance." EPS is a number that is watched obsessively by investors and analysts, and so is often crucial to share performance--but it is also easy to manipulate.

It was becoming harder and harder for Enron to deliver growth in EPS, so its "laser" focused on looking for accounting devices to make it appear that EPS was going up, and also to remove debt from its books. Thus a large number of off-balance-sheet entities were set up, which were not wholly independent of Enron, but were judged sufficiently separate that the profit and loss did not have to be considered part of Enron's results. Through a process known as "securitization," certain assets, or portfolios of assets, were then "sold" to these entities, in return for Enron stock, or loans guaranteed by Enron stock. Some of the partnership deals required Enron to pay millions of dollars if its stock price fell below a certain point, which became important later. Securitization is a legally approved financial device, used by many business firms--not just by Enron--in recent years to increase return on investment without having to report debt on its balance sheet. But the transactions must be valued correctly, and in order for the transfers with the off-balance sheet SPE's to be considered separate from Enron (and thus off the books), the SPE's must be at least 3% owned by one or more outside investors. (*The Rise and Fall of Enron,* Journal of Accountancy, April 2002).

It appears that even this minimal level of outside investment was not always met in the SPEs, with Enron stock or pledges of stock accounting for part of the 3%. Sometimes swaps were created on Enron's balance sheet that would compensate the buyer of assets in the event of unexpected loss. Sometimes the third party would pay using a loan from Enron, which then booked the interest on the loan as income. For non-liquid assets, Enron had considerable discretion in deciding what constituted a fair price.

While Enron had a huge trading business—it was the largest energy trader in North America—its success led dozens of rivals to enter the field. And although its total revenues were growing rapidly, its profit margins were consistently shrinking. Its trading margins declined from 5.3% in early 1998 to less than 1.7% in the third quarter of 2001, noted the investment firm Reed Wasden. As analyst Cary Wasden stated, "margins have fallen in spite of the company's practice of selling fixed assets (such as power generation plants) and booking the gains as operating income."

Enron also may have inflated its profits by lumping sales of assets such as pipelines into its trading business. In fact, profits from hard assets may have masked the shrinking margins of Mr. Skilling's virtual trading business and encouraged him to bet the company on his radical, risky view that Enron could create markets in just about anything. As margins shrank, Skilling stretched into new areas. Enron grew to have contracts with some 8,000 counterparts, in hundreds of business lines ranging from credit insurance to metals trading, and even bigger risks, such as trading telecoms bandwidth.

Based on the strength of its highflying shares, Enron executives were able to convince investors, bankers, analysts, accountants, debt-rating agencies and even Enron's own employees that its promise was real, and its growth never-ending. As *New York Times* writer Gretchen Morgenson has commented, "Enron's executives were surely smart enough to know that once they had convinced bankers, brokers and accountants of the company's strength, all parties could pretty much be counted on to keep the myth of solidarity alive, even after problems arose. When questions were first raised about partnerships that should have been listed in financial statements, true believers could be relied on to drown out naysayers." (*New York Times*, Jan. 14, 2001)

Wall Street firms were generating millions of dollars selling Enron's shares and bonds to investors, and analysts were among the most vociferous defenders of the company, even as its stock price fell during 2001. Indeed, David Fleischer, who followed Enron for Goldman, Sachs, recommended it until October 17, the day after Enron disclosed that it had lost $618 million in the most recent quarter (admitting that earlier financial statements had been inaccurate), and that it was cutting $1.2 billion off its previously reported net worth. Lehman Brothers continued to rate Enron a strong buy even after October. Why? Everyone was making lots of money.

The Downward Spiral in the Last Half of 2001

During the summer of 2001, Enron vice-president Sherron Watkins was working for CFO Andrew Fastow, attempting to find assets to sell to help Enron's financial picture. However, everywhere she looked she ran into off-the-books arrangements that no one could explain or wanted to investigate. She knew that other people who had pressed Mr. Skilling for explanations had been transferred to other positions within Enron. Ms. Watkins discovered that Enron was losing substantial money on two equity investments, but that the losses were not appearing in the company's public filings. Watkins, a CPA with a masters degree in accounting (who had formerly worked for Arthur Andersen), was troubled. "The numbers just didn't add up," she said.

When Mr. Skilling suddenly resigned as CEO on August 14, Ms. Watkins' concerns increased, as did that of many Enron employees. Mr. Lay called an all-employees meeting two days later to reassure them that all was well, that the company was in fine shape, and he asked employees to send him letters if there was anything they thought he should know. Ms. Watkins wrote a one-page anonymous letter and dropped it off before the meeting, detailing her concerns. Then after hearing Mr. Lay's upbeat speech, she wrote a detailed 6-page letter (in her own name) describing her reservations about the lack of disclosure of the off-balance sheet SPEs funded by Enron and operated by Mr. Fastow. She concluded her memo by stating her fear that the company might "implode under a series of accounting scandals." She personally met with Mr. Lay a few days later and discussed these issues with him. Mr. Lay notified Enron's attorneys, the large law firm of Vinson & Elkins, and its auditors Arthur Andersen and asked for their opinions. A few weeks later Vinson & Elkins reported that after its investigation, there were no serious problems and suggested that a deeper investigation was not warranted.

It is now clear that the investigation of the Watkins memo charges was just another chapter in a behind-the-scenes struggle which had been ongoing for at least five years between Vinson & Elkins (V & E), often represented by partner Ronald Astin, and Enron CFO Andrew Fastow. These discussions concerned how much information it was necessary to disclose concerning the many off-book SPEs created and funded by Enron, and the conflicts of interest that were present in such business deals. At that time, Enron was V & E's largest client, paying the law firm $35.6 million in 2001, although Enron also used several other outside law firms. From 1997, when Enron proposed the first off-book partnership, there were numerous occasions when Mr. Astin or other V & E lawyers would raise objections about the lack of disclosure concerning, and conflicts of interest inherent in the off-book deals, only to be met with opposition and arguments from Mr. Fastow and other Enron officials.

Sometimes after these difficult discussions, Vinson & Elkins would go ahead and draw up the necessary partnership documents. On other occasions, Enron would just go ahead with the deal, in spite of Mr. Astin's advice that a particular transaction was a conflict of interest. Occasionally Enron would go to other law firms for advice, if unsatisfied with the answers from Vinson & Elkins. Enron was the client, after all, and could accept or reject the advice of counsel. On all occasions the legal advice given by V&E was provided either directly to the Enron officers or Enron's in-house counsel, per its agreement with the firm. It does not appear that Vinson & Elkins or Mr. Astin ever went directly to the Enron board of directors to discuss its concerns about the off-book partnerships.

Mr. Lay was finally forced to announce on October 16, 2001 that Enron was taking a $35 million charge against earnings to reflect losses on the off-book partnerships, that Enron had lost $618 million in the 3rd quarter, and that Enron was also reducing equity capital by $1.2 billion, stemming from a hedging deal with another off-balance sheet set of entities called "Raptors." Later in October, Mr. Fastow, the architect of the controversial private partnerships—two of which were named LJM and LJM2 for the initials of his wife and children—was removed from his position and placed on leave. The company then restated its accounts for the past five years, in the process wiping out nearly $600 million of profits (about 1/5 of the total). These moves started a free fall in the value of Enron's shares.

Once investors and analysts started to doubt that Enron was profitable, its survival became an immediate issue. Suddenly its lack of financial candor was creating problems. Enron had been able to receive seemingly endless loans because its debt was rated investment grade. However, many of the loans had clauses requiring Enron to make substantial additional payments if its credit rating was downgraded. And many of the off-sheet partnerships (SPEs) had clauses requiring Enron to pay millions of dollars on demand if the share price fell below a certain value. News and rumors of Enron's severe financial troubles caused the Securities and Exchange Commission to open a formal inquiry into Enron on October 31.

When customers of Enron and its trading partners began to lose confidence in the company, its trading business began to dry up. Even after the start of the SEC investigation, Enron still refused to fully acknowledge its financial problems. Mr. Lay desperately sought help from his political friends in Washington. In late October, he called Commerce Secretary Donald Evans, one of President Bush's closest friends, well known to Mr. Lay. However, Mr. Evans was out of town. Mr. Lay then called Treasury Secretary Paul O'Neill, at his Washington DC apartment. Mr. Lay described Enron's desperate problems, suggesting that the company collapse could put the entire financial system at risk. Mr. O'Neill said he would look into the situation. A few days later, Mr. Evans and Mr. O'Neill met at the Treasury Department a weekly economic meeting. The two men mentioned they had each heard from Mr. Lay but both decided not to intervene.

As more and more debts were called due, Enron's share price declined to $15/share in early November. After a series of talks, Enron reached tentative agreement with a smaller energy trading rival, Dynegy Co. on a merger on November 7. This deal would have infused an additional $1.5 billion of badly needed cash into Enron. However, on Nov. 19, Enron filed its quarterly SEC 10-Q report, which revealed that it had spent $2 billion since the merger was announced, and could not account for where most of the money had gone. Furthermore, the report noted that payment on an overdue note had been accelerated, and Enron thus owed another $690 million, due in a few days. Dynegy executives, who had not been told of either of these matters, were outraged. Although several lengthy negotiating sessions were held, both in Houston and New York over the next two weeks in an attempt to resuscitate the merger, eventually Dynegy called off the deal.

On December 2, 2001 Enron filed for protection under Chapter 11 of the Bankruptcy code. (*Enron's Many Strands: The Company Unravels,* New York Times, Feb. 10, 2002) Enron stock was now selling at $0.26/share, and Mr. Lay resigned as chair a few weeks later. Enron's debt of $13.1 billion plus another $18 billion for its affiliates was the largest corporate bankruptcy in American history. Creditors, shareholders, lenders and others who were owed money by Enron now had to do battle within the confines of bankruptcy court, and those struggles are ongoing. Many shareholder lawsuits have been filed against Enron, and a Justice Department criminal investigation was opened in mid-2002.

Arthur Andersen LLP

History of the Firm

The accounting firm Arthur Andersen LLP (limited liability partnership) was first established in 1913 as Andersen, Delany & Co. in Chicago. The founder, Arthur Andersen, was a professor at Northwestern University. In 1918 the firm's name became simply Arthur Andersen & Co. In 1947 Mr. Andersen died, and the firm almost dissolved. However, Leonard Spacek, a close associate of Mr. Andersen, was able to hold the company together and his leadership from 1947 to 1963 helped propel Andersen to the top of its profession. The firm began to undertake business consulting in the late 1940s. The first international office, in Mexico City, was opened in 1955 and five offices were opened in Europe during Spacek's tenure. Andersen expanded to Hong Kong and Singapore in 1972 in other Asian countries shortly thereafter. After Enron was formed by the merger of Houston Natural Gas and InterNorth in 1985, Arthur Andersen was hired as its auditor.

Over the years, Anderson grew to become one of the largest accounting firms in the world. In 1979, according to the Andersen website, "Arthur Andersen became the world's largest professional services firm" with "more than 1,000 partners." As with the other huge global accounting firms, management consulting increasingly occupied a larger place within the profit structure of the business than the traditional functions of accounting and auditing. The growth of nonaudit business lines at all the Big Five led to considerable criticism, most pointedly in the late 1990s by Arthur Levitt, then chairman of the Securities and Exchange Commission. He urged that the auditing function be separated from the management consulting practice, warning that accountants would inevitably be swayed from delivering harsh audits by the prospect of losing large consulting fees if their audits were too strict.

At Arthur Andersen, in particular, the tension between the accounting division and the more profitable consulting arm became increasingly acute during the 1980s. Andersen split its accounting and consulting sides into two separate units in 1989. "There were pressures within Andersen to step up the profitability of the accounting, audit, tax, whatever else was there. . . to match the profitability of Andersen Consulting," said Duane R. Kullberg, who was the firm's chief executive at the time. After a number of contentious years, the two sides split completely in 2000, following a hard-fought 3-year arbitration proceeding between the accounting unit (Arthur Andersen) and the consulting side (Andersen Consulting, which then became a separate firm called Accenture). Arthur Andersen hoped to get as much as $15 billion in separation payments from Andersen Consulting, but received only $1 billion, putting more pressure on the accountants to bring in more revenue. (*Lone Ranger of Auditors Fell Slowly Out of Saddle,* New York Times, April 20, 2002).

The Traditions of the Firm Begin to Change

Throughout its history, Arthur Andersen had been known for its independence, and for its insistence on full and complete financial disclosure, despite the occasional resistance of its clients. Indeed, Andersen's website proudly proclaims, as the second item in a 3-page company "Timeline," that in 1915 Arthur Andersen himself took the position that a Great Lakes steamship company must reflect in its balance sheet the economic impact of a post-year end event of major proportions (the sinking of a freighter). "This marks the first time an auditor demanded the disclosure of such an event (occurring after yearend but before issuance of the auditor's report) in order to ensure accurate reporting," states the website notation. Andersen partners sometimes were described as "arrogant" by competitors due to the rectitude with which its partners carried themselves. "A lot of that came from Arthur Andersen himself," said Arthur Bowman, editor of Bowman's Accounting Report. Mr. Andersen was known to stand by whatever he thought was the proper accounting approach, no matter what.

However, in the new climate of the 1990s the firm began to change, as the cost of saying "no" to a paying client rose considerably. By 2001, Andersen and its worldwide affiliates employed some 85,000 people in 84 countries, with more than 28,000 employees and partners in the United States. Andersen's 2001 revenue in the U.S. was $9.3 billion. However, increasing competition and the need for even greater revenue was causing the accountants and auditors to face tremendous pressure to sign off on clients' financial disclosures, even though some items were questionable. The focus of management changed more to "How can we enhance our topline revenues, even at the cost of conceding on quality," said Arthur Wyatt, a former Andersen partner who now teaches at the University of Illinois. "Not knowingly doing a bad job, but knowingly accepting an accounting practice of a client that was questionable at best." (*Id.*)

During the latter part of 2001, as Enron stock plummeted in value and the company eventually filed for Chapter 11 bankruptcy, various Enron creditors and investors as well as government agencies began to look at the role Arthur Andersen LLP. Over the years, Andersen had performed extensive professional services for Enron, and had helped prepare Enron's records and certified hundreds of financial statements of Enron. If indeed, the success of Enron had been built upon inaccurate and misleading financial records, why were those records continuously approved by Andersen?

The Relationship Between Arthur Andersen and Enron

What has emerged through the spotlight of media and press coverage in recent months was that Arthur Andersen had become much more than an independent auditor of the financial records of Enron, and was much closer to a partner. Unlike an old-fashioned audit, in which accountants rigorously review financial records, invoices, receipts, billings and more, and only then sign off on a client's financial statements, Andersen developed a system that combined this external role with the "internal audit"-- the company's own review of its books. And Andersen mingled both of those functions with consulting services. "Out here, we don't call audit, audit," said Patricia Grutzmacher, an Andersen auditor working in Enron's offices. In order to help sell the "integrated-audit" model to its own staffers and other potential clients, Andersen made a series of videos between 1998 and early 2001 extolling the virtues of the system. "They understand what we need and are making sure that we get that," said Enron's Jeffrey Skilling in one video. Enron chief accounting officer Rick Causey (who had been with Arthur Andersen for 9 years before joining Enron) said in another video, "We expect them to be here and to be able to be responsive to our needs...hopefully even being able to reach the conclusions we want." (*On Camera, People at Andersen, Enron Tell How Close They Were,* Wall St. Journal, April 15, 2002)

Andersen was providing constant advice regarding the keeping of the records, helping with the creation of the off-book partnerships and "securitization" of assets, and assisting in the development of the sophisticated accounting techniques necessitated by

Enron's increasingly varied and speculative trading practices. In fact, Arthur Andersen leased office space within the Enron headquarters building (which occupied one whole floor) and had 100 employees there, so that Andersen's Houston office and Enron were essentially together in "real time." By this time Enron had become one of Arthur Andersen's three largest clients, paying Andersen a total of $54 million in 2000 for auditing and consulting services--slightly more than $1 million per week.

On a number of occasions during 1999 and 2000 various Andersen partners questioned Enron's financial practices, which led to internal battles within the accounting firm. One Andersen partner, Carl Bass, was removed from monitoring Enron after he had raised objections to its practices, particularly with respect to the group of special purpose entities (SPEs) known as the Raptors. It appears that Enron officials complained to Andersen executives about Mr. Bass, and requested that he be replaced on the Enron account. In other instances, Arthur Andersen's Professional Standards Group (based in Chicago), which is responsible for resolving difficult accounting questions faced by the firm nationwide, had criticized some of the financial and accounting practices used by Enron, and had made recommendations for change --but the criticism was apparently ignored by Andersen's Houston office.

The "Document Retention" Memo and the Shredding of Documents

As Enron crumbled and hurtled toward bankruptcy in late 2001, it was becoming clear that many lawsuits were going to be filed against Enron, and also that Congress and various government agencies were going to conduct thorough investigations into the financial and other aspects of the Enron debacle. About this time an important memo was sent from an attorney at Arthur Andersen's headquarters in Chicago to the Andersen Houston office. On October 12, Andersen attorney Nancy Temple sent an e-mail to the Houston office reminding them of, and urging them to comply with Arthur Andersen's "document retention" policy. Among others, the memo was received by David Duncan, the lead Andersen partner on the Enron account.

Nearly 2 weeks later, on October 23, after Andersen had learned that the SEC had launched a preliminary investigation into Enron's accounting and financial disclosures, Mr. Duncan held a meeting to discuss implementing the document policy. He interpreted the memo from Ms. Temple as a signal to start destroying Enron documents and other potential evidence of improper financial dealings. Mr. Duncan proceeded to initiate a wholesale and massive shredding program, during which what one investigator later called "tons and tons" of documents in the Arthur Andersen offices related to Enron were destroyed and thousands of e-mail files deleted, over the next few weeks. The Andersen document shredding machines were running non-stop, with documents arriving in the shredding room in scores of trunks and boxes, while secretaries waited in a long line at the shredder. Frustrated with waiting, they hired a courier and shipped 20 or 30 trunks of documents to the main Andersen Houston offices, some 6 blocks away, where they were shredded.

Mr. Duncan communicated with Andersen offices in Portland and London as well, regarding the need to follow the "document retention" policy. In three days of shredding in Houston, some 26 trunks of documents and 24 boxes, were shredded-- compared with less than one trunk's worth being shredded in each of the previous three weeks. There was also a threefold increase in the volume of e-mail deletions. The shredding slowed down after a few days, and finally stopped when the SEC upgraded its inquiry to a formal investigation. On November 8, Andersen received a subpoena from the SEC. The next day Mr. Duncan's secretary sent out a mass e-mail which said "Stop the shredding." *(Andersen Misread Depths of the Government's Anger*, New York Times, March 18, 2002)

Arthur Andersen's Responses to The Shredding Fiasco

In January 2002 Congress started holding hearings on the Enron debacle, and the top officers at Arthur Andersen began searching for records and e-mail files to help prepare its partners for their inevitable Congressional testimony. Only then did the top officials learn about the massive shredding of documents in the Houston office during the past October. They discovered that many important records and files relating to Enron were missing. In a conference call on January 4, Andersen general counsel Andrew Pincus reported on a series of interviews he had done with employees in the Houston office. Mr. Pincus found that the e-mail deletions and the shredding had been done on a scale that was both abnormal and suspicious.

After a flurry of meetings and telephone calls, the top Andersen executives decided they needed to act quickly. Knowing that Mr. Duncan, the Andersen partner and the lead auditor on the Enron account, was meeting with SEC investigators within a few days, Andersen notified officials with the SEC, the Justice Department, and Congress on January 10 that the Houston office had destroyed "a significant, but undetermined number" of documents related to Enron. By openly admitting that mistakes had been made, Andersen hoped to quiet the issue, but instead the announcement created a firestorm, as many clients called to say that their concerns were heightened by the disclosure, and demanded to know more. At that point Mr. Duncan hired a New York law firm to represent him. A few days later, while at his lawyer's office, he was interviewed by telephone for 20 minutes by Andersen's lawyers. A few days later, Andersen fired Mr. Duncan, based upon his role in the document destruction. With the topic of massive "document shredding" hitting the front pages of national newspapers, Andersen tried to respond.

Joseph Berardino, then Chairman of Andersen Worldwide, had believed for some time that Andersen needed to establish some sort of independent board, to better police itself, and now he pushed the idea aggressively, meeting with current SEC chairman Harvey Pitt and former SEC chairman Arthur Levitt. During his tenure at the SEC during the 1990s, Mr. Levitt had urged that certain reforms be made in accounting industry practices (which reforms had been bitterly opposed by Arthur Andersen and the other leading firms--as well as by Mr. Pitt, who then was representing several of the "Big Five" firms). Mr. Levitt liked the idea of an independent board, but refused to serve personally. He and others suggested that Andersen contact Paul A. Volcker, the 75-year old highly respected former chairman of the Federal Reserve Board. Mr. Berardino quickly met with Mr. Volcker, who agreed to become involved, but only if he was granted the extraordinary power to dictate changes in the way the firm did business. Mr. Berardino agreed with Mr. Volcker's terms a few days later.

By then Andersen had been named as a defendant in several civil suits filed by Enron creditors and investors, alleging negligence and malpractice in its work auditing Enron's financial records. With public pressure and media interest increasing from the document destruction scandal, Andersen desperately wanted to settle the civil suits. An investment banking firm hired by Andersen determined that by combining its assets, future earnings and insurance proceeds, Andersen could afford to pay $750 million to settle the suits. The SEC and some creditors seemed impressed, but William Lerach, a well-known plaintiffs' lawyer who was appointed lead counsel in the suits, said that the number was not nearly large enough. (*Miscues, Missteps and the Fall of Andersen*, New York Times, May 7, 2002)

The Justice Department Files Criminal Charges

While Andersen was devoting efforts to settle the civil suits in February 2002, the United States Justice Department was considering filing criminal "obstruction of justice" charges against Arthur Andersen, as the result of the massive document destruction. Andersen lawyers met personally on March 3 with the Justice Department lawyers to discuss the situation. Robert Fiske Jr., a partner at Davis Polk & Wardwell, made the first presentation for Andersen. While he acknowledged that inappropriate behavior (document destruction) had been done, he argued that this was surely the action of individuals, not the whole firm. An indictment of Arthur Andersen LLP as a firm was unwarranted, he said, would be a death blow, as clients would abandon the firm, and its business would unwind.

However, the government's top lawyer was unconvinced. Michael Chertoff (deputy attorney general and head of the criminal division) responded to Andersen's last attempt to derail the charges in a two-page letter, forcefully describing the document destruction as part of a chain of misdeeds that, taken together, ultimately demanded that criminal charges be filed. Among other things, Mr. Chertoff wrote, the document destruction in the Enron case came just months after Arthur Andersen had entered into an agreement with the S.E.C. arising out of an accounting fraud investigation involving another Andersen client, Waste Management Inc. As part of that settlement, Andersen had signed a consent decree promising not to commit misdeeds in the future. According to Mr. Chertoff, Andersen's actions with regard to Enron had clearly violated its "probation." Mr. Chertoff also stated that, in this case, the document destruction was not committed because of some benign motive. "The conduct here was not the isolated act of a few low-level employees acting out of panic or engaging in misjudgment," he wrote. The Justice Department announced the indictment on March 14.

Over the next two weeks, Andersen officials and lawyers held many discussions with government prosecutors, trying to come up with a way of reaching a plea agreement or some other settlement on the criminal charges. Various options, including an admission of "wrongdoing" by Andersen without admitting "guilt" to criminal charges, and other possible resolutions were vigorously debated between the parties, but no agreement was reached. However, talks regarding a settlement continued, with the government insisting on some sort of a guilty plea by Andersen, or at least an admission of wrongdoing, plus extensive cooperation on other cases.

While these events were occurring, Arthur Andersen's business was declining, and the firm began to actively explore a merger with other accounting firms. Serious negotiations were undertaken with Deloitte & Touche, and exploratory talks took place with other members of the Big Five, but stalled on various issues, the most serious being the potential liability that the second firm might acquire, due to malpractice by Andersen. Meanwhile, Mr. Lerach, upon learning of these discussions, demanded that any buyers of Andersen kick in at least $1 billion toward settlement of the pending civil claims, which clearly none of the potential buyer firms wanted to do. Then in April, Mr. Duncan, the lead Andersen auditor for Enron, agreed to personally plead guilty to obstruction of justice charges, and to testify against Andersen at trial. This caused the prosecutors to demand even greater concessions from Andersen. None of the matters was settled, and the federal criminal case was set for trial. Andersen had become the first major accounting firm ever charged with a felony. A conviction could carry up to a $500,000 fine and five years probation. More importantly, a finding of guilt would bar the firm form auditing public companies.

The Criminal Trial Against Arthur Andersen

The federal criminal trial began on May 6, 2002. The charge against Andersen was "obstruction of justice" based primarily on the allegation that the massive document shredding and record destruction had occurred with the knowledge and belief that an SEC investigation of the firm was imminent. The charge stated that officers and managers of

— the firm Arthur Andersen LLP "did knowingly, intentionally and corruptly persuade and attempt to persuade other persons, to wit: Andersen partners and employees" to withhold records, documents and other objects from an official proceeding. The prosecution's allegations included the following statement:

Instead of being advised to preserve documentation so as to assist Enron and the SEC, Andersen employees on the Enron engagement team were instructed by Andersen partners and others to destroy immediately documentation relating to Enron, and told to work overtime if necessary to accomplish the destruction. During the next few weeks, an unparalleled initiative was undertaken to shred physical documentation and delete computer files. Tons of paper relating to the Enron audit were promptly shredded as part of the orchestrated document destruction. The shredder at the Andersen office in the Enron building was used virtually constantly and, to handle the overload, dozens of large trunks filled with Enron documents were sent to Andersen's main Houston office to be shredded.

Three weeks after the trial began, the prosecution wrapped up its case on May 27. Prosecution witnesses included Securities and Exchange Commission investigators, FBI agents and other government regulators, as well as present and past Andersen staff members. The defense team responded by presenting its evidence for 6 days. The case was given to the jury on June 5, following 21 days of testimony. The government was allowed by Judge Melinda Harmon to introduce evidence of Andersen's past "bad acts," including its consent decree with the SEC in June 2001 regarding charges that it had issued false and misleading reports on behalf of Waste Management, Inc. In that case, Andersen had agreed to pay a $7 million fine and had signed a promise not to violate the law in the future, on penalty of being held in contempt of court. Prosecutors sought to use this evidence now because it provided a motive for the massive Enron shredding--an attempt to cover up evidence which would show that Andersen had violated its previous agreement with the SEC.

Defense attorney Rusty Hardin, a veteran Houston trial lawyer, vigorously answered by calling the case "one of the greatest tragedies of the criminal justice system." Mr. Hardin portrayed Andersen as a "proud firm" with a long and distinguished history and argued that the entire firm's 28,000 employees and partners should not be made to suffer because of poor judgment by a few members. In his opening statement, Mr. Hardin repeatedly compared the prosecutors' case to the children's book "Where's Waldo?" because the indictment had not indicated who within Andersen specifically "corruptly influenced" others to break the law. Mr. Hardin's colorful language and antics often livened up the trial, as did his frequent clashes with Judge Harmon over her rulings. (*Andersen Hits Major Setback One Day Into Criminal Trial,* Wall St. Journal, May 8, 2002)

The star witness for the prosecution was David Duncan, the former Andersen partner who had pleaded guilty earlier to obstructing justice in connection with the shredding of Enron-related documents. Mr. Duncan testified that, "On or about October 19, 2001 we learned of a Securities and Exchange Commission investigation. On October 23 I instructed local people at Arthur Andersen to begin destroying documents, with the knowledge and intent that those documents would be unavailable to the SEC and others." Mr. Duncan also admitted that he had worried back in fall 2001 that the questionable Enron accounting and approval of all the "off-book" partnerships could lead to a regulatory probe and possible shareholder lawsuits.

However, in his answers to questions on cross-examination Mr. Duncan stated that he could remember only one specific document that he had destroyed and that he had not tried to get other recipients of the documents to destroy their own copies of those same documents. Mr. Duncan also testified that he "was not thinking about Waste Management" when he gave the orders to begin the mass shredding of files, which undercut one of the main prosecution theories. And Mr. Duncan stated that he did not believe he was breaking the law back in October, but only came to that conclusion after much "soul searching," considerable reading of the law, and reflection earlier this year.

Judge Harmon's instructions to the jury directed them to answer the question: "Did at least one agent of Andersen--either a partner, officer or employee--try to "corruptly persuade" another person to keep a document from being available "for use in an official proceeding?" The phrase "corruptly persuade" was defined by Judge Harmon as acting with an "improper purpose," such as "intent to subvert or undermine the fact-finding ability of an official proceeding" (the informal and formal investigations by the SEC, for example). Although the government needed to prove only that one Andersen person did all these things, attorney Hardin vigorously cross-examined the prosecution witnesses regarding exactly who, within Andersen, was the "corrupt persuader." "Where's Waldo," he kept asking. Obviously Mr. Duncan was the most important and likely "persuader," since he had admitted, under oath, that he was guilty of obstruction of justice. But Mr. Hardin's cross examination raised the possibility that jurors might believe that Mr. Duncan's "soul searching" confession was largely based on his fear of facing serious jail time if he did not cooperate, as well as the possibility of additional prosecutions on more serious crimes.

The Jury Reaches a Verdict

After receiving a 12-page list of Jury Instructions from Judge Melinda Harmon regarding the law to be applied, the twelve-member jury deliberated for 10 days. They were "sequestered," which means they were required to stay at a hotel in downtown Houston. After about one week of deliberations, the jury sent a note to the judge indicating that the members were deadlocked, and the possibility of a "hung jury" (reaching no verdict) seemed likely. Judge Harmon urged the jury to "Redouble your efforts" and keep trying to reach a verdict in order to spare both sides the agony and expense of another trial. The next day the jury sent another note to Judge Harmon asking whether they could find Andersen guilty if they all believed that someone at Andersen had violated the law, but could not agree as to one particular person. Judge Harmon answered the next day that although this was a case of "first impression," (no valid legal precedents to rely on) they could indeed convict under such circumstances, a ruling which clearly favored the prosecution.

The jury finally reached a decision on June 15, finding the accounting firm Arthur Andersen "Guilty" on one count of Obstruction of Justice. The jury also stated that they did unanimously agree that one particular person within Andersen had attempted to obstruct justice, thus decreasing the importance of Judge Harmon's last ruling. The verdict represented the first felony conviction of a major accounting firm--as the felony indictment had also been the first such event. The judge set sentencing for October 11, 2002, at which time Andersen could be fined up to $500,000. The most severe penalty, however, is that SEC rules will prohibit Andersen from performing audits of public companies. Within hours of the verdict, Arthur Andersen announced that it would voluntarily cease auditing public companies by the end of August, thus effectively ending the life of the firm. Although Andersen immediately said that an appeal would be filed, it is expected to be at least one year before the appellate hearing will take place, and by that time there will be little left of the firm.

Four members of the jury held a press conference after the verdict was announced. They stated that when deliberations first began, an initial poll of the jury indicated that they were evenly split 6-6 on guilt or acquittal. Gradually, over the next week to 10 days, as they meticulously reviewed the testimony of various witnesses, considered many pieces of evidence, and debated the meaning of the judge's instructions, more jury members began to lean toward a conviction. Despite hearing a number of witnesses testify about Andersen's massive document shredding and the deletion of thousands of e-mail messages related to Enron, several members of the jury commented that neither the paper shredding, nor the testimony of lead auditor David Duncan (who had individually pleaded guilty to obstruction of justice) were key factors in reaching their decision.

The jurors who met with the press indicated that the most decisive evidence leading to their decision was one e-mail message sent to Mr. Duncan by Andersen attorney Nancy Temple. This message consisted of comments and suggested changes in a "memo to the file" prepared by Mr. Duncan recounting his disagreement with the Enron accounting department concerning certain financial statements--as described more fully below. This jury revelation surprised most observers, because neither the prosecution nor defense had placed much focus on that particular e-mail during the trial. In the end the jury apparently found (while not explicitly naming the person) that Ms. Temple, not Mr. Duncan was the "corrupt persuader" (necessary under Judge Harmon's instructions) whose actions forced them to find Arthur Andersen guilty.

The background for Ms. Temple's important e-mail message was the increasing concern at Arthur Andersen over Enron's financial problems in fall 2001. As events at Enron unfolded and media and public interest in Enron's finances increased, members of the Andersen audit team in Houston consulted with, and later sent several memorandums to the accounting specialists (the Professional Standards Group) at Andersen headquarters in Chicago, discussing the Enron off-book partnerships known as Raptors. The Chicago staff found that the memos from the Houston office did not accurately reflect their advice and consultations, or their view that Enron's accounting procedures had violated the accounting profession's "Generally Accepted Accounting Principles." By late September, Enron's problems had become critical, and the legal department at Andersen's Chicago headquarters became more directly involved with Andersen's role in Enron's financial problems. The matter was assigned to Ms. Temple, a fairly new member of the legal department. Ms. Temple, 38, had graduated from Harvard Law School, and had become a successful litigator and partner at a large and prestigious Chicago law firm before joining Arthur Andersen.

In mid-October as the news media and government agencies were becoming more interested in Enron, Ms. Temple reminded several other members and offices of Arthur Andersen of the firm's "document retention policy" (what to keep and what to throw away) in a series of conference calls, and also told the members of Andersen's Enron team in Houston that "it would be helpful" if they made sure they were in compliance with the policy, and that extraneous records should be destroyed. The massive shredding of documents began shortly thereafter. However, despite considerable testimony about these events at trial, the jury chose to focus on another event.

At about this same time Ms. Temple reviewed a draft of an internal memorandum prepared by David Duncan, Andersen's lead partner on the Enron account. In the memo, Mr. Duncan described a conversation he had recently had with Richard Causey, Enron's accounting chief, concerning a news release that Enron was planning to issue regarding its $1 billion 3rd quarter charge to earnings, reflecting investment losses. The Enron press release described such losses as "non-recurring," although accounting rules regard such losses as a normal part of the calculation of profits and losses. Mr. Duncan and other Andersen auditors believed that Enron's representation was "misleading," and thus did not accurately reflect current earnings/losses.

Mr. Duncan told Causey that such misleading information issued by other companies had provided the basis for previous S.E.C. investigations, and he recorded this thought in the draft internal memo, a copy of which he sent to Ms. Temple. Shortly thereafter, Ms. Temple sent an e-mail reply to Mr. Duncan suggesting that he remove that portion from his final memo "to protect ourselves" from SEC scrutiny. "I suggest deleting some language that might suggest we have concluded the release is misleading," she wrote. Ms. Temple also suggested deleting any reference to consultation with the

Andersen headquarters legal staff and ask that Duncan "delete my name" from the memo. Mr. Duncan did in fact delete the requested items from his final memorandum.

The jury foreman, Oscar Criner, a computer science professor at Texas Southern University, referred to that memo as a "smoking gun" and said that the jury had concluded that Ms. Temple knew that the SEC was going to investigate and that her intent in the memo was therefore to keep information from the SEC. Thus she had acted to "corruptly persuade" Mr. Duncan to alter information in order to impede the impending SEC investigation. This provided proof of the important element of "obstruction of justice" that Judge Harmon told the jurors was necessary in order to convict Arthur Andersen. Indeed, it appears that Mr. Criner himself was the last holdout among the jury members. He had argued against a conviction (the next to last vote was 11-1) until persuaded--after reviewing Judge Harmon's instructions--that Ms. Temple was trying to "corruptly persuade" others to change documents to hinder the upcoming SEC investigation. The first Duncan memorandum showed that Andersen officials did not agree with the wording of the Enron press release regarding "non-recurring" losses. When Enron ignored Andersen's advice and issued the press release anyway, "Arthur Andersen set about to alter documents to keep that away from the SEC," stated the jury foreman, Prof. Criner (who intends to write a book about the case). Thus the jury found that the necessary elements of obstruction of justice were met, and a conviction was required.

After the verdict, Samuel Buell, assistant U.S. attorney stated, "The verdict sends a message out loud and clear to the accounting industry to get their priorities straight." Andrew Weissmann, another lead prosecutor stated that the case boiled down to a simple principle: "When you expect the police, you don't destroy the evidence." Mr. Weissmann said that employees and others upset about the firm's collapse should "look to Andersen management for responsibility." He pointed out that Andersen had already faced litigation in recent years from the SEC over accounting failures involving other clients such as Sunbeam Corporation and Waste Management, Inc. "This was a management team that already had two strikes against them, and they refused to take this situation seriously," he said.

Andersen officials saw the result differently. C. E. Andrews, a senior partner at the firm said, "We do not regret going to trial. The purpose of this was to fight for our honor and dignity. We do not believe we committed a crime." Andersen attorney Rusty Hardin commented that the jury had actually rejected the government's primary accusations--that Andersen had destroyed thousands of records to impede the SEC inquiry. "They convicted on a theory that wasn't even argued by the government," he said. Andersen's assertions of innocence (what one New York Times commentator described as its "lack of contrition") continued unabated, as the firm issued a statement following the verdict blaming the Justice Department for what had happened. "It is clear that the government failed to uphold its moral responsibility to the public by indicting and prosecuting a firm of 26,000 innocent people...and destroying the firm as we knew it," said the Andersen statement.

The Andersen decision is hardly the end of the story. Following the verdict, Deputy United States Attorney General Larry Thompson stated that, "This prosecution has been but one piece of our active and ongoing investigation into the circumstances behind the collapse of Enron." The head of the Justice Department's Enron task force, Leslie Caldwell, suggested that further cases--including criminal actions against Andersen executives--could be ahead. "We are still looking at everything. We're not finished with Arthur Andersen," she said. There is currently a grand jury looking into possible criminal activity by Enron and its executives, and the SEC stated, "The Commission's investigation into Enron Corp. and Andersen's role in it is continuing."

The Break-up of Arthur Andersen

Since the indictment of Arthur Andersen, much of the activity taking place within Andersen offices has not concerned accounting and auditing, but discussions of where the Andersen partners and employees might be going, and with whom they will be working in the future. In the months since the indictment of the firm on March 14, the firm has lost many of its long-time clients, and many employees. The firm was fighting for its life, but after the guilty verdict, the battle will undoubtedly be lost. During the spring, Andersen stated that it hoped to remain in business, as an auditing and accounting firm only. A layoff of 7,000 of its 28,000 U.S. employees was announced on April 8. Those who still were working at Andersen in the summer of 2002 were spending considerable time looking for other employment. The former president of Andersen Worldwide, Joseph Berardino, who resigned on March 26, had stated that after the indictment he had turned his attention to finding jobs for the firm's employees. "I've become the chief placement officer for 85,000 people. The Hartford, Conn. Office actually held a job fair within its offices, so employees could interview with other financial services firms. (*Andersen: A Shadow of its Former Self*, Wall St. Journal, 4-30-02)

In the U.S., where Andersen had 1,750 partners, the firm has either reached tentative agreements or is in talks with rivals that would cover 1,200 partners. The situation remains extremely fluid with no definitive deal as yet. Potential acquirers continue to worry about possible successor liability, with lawyers trying to determine the fine line between hiring staff, and acquiring parts of a business. Meanwhile, what actually may be acquired if another firm purchases a part of Arthur Andersen diminishes each day as more clients leave and individual partners negotiate deals on their own.

For each Andersen partner hired by a rival firm, Andersen expected roughly 10 staff members of all levels to go along and for the buyer to pay between $100,000 and $150,000 in exchange for obtaining a release from the partner's noncompete agreement, which would otherwise prevent the partner from doing work for a former Andersen client. In return, the buyers would get the partner's client list. Indeed between the indictment and the trial, Andersen lost 270 of its 2,300 public company clients in the U.S, and since the guilty verdict, they are all looking elsewhere. In many other cases, companies are waiting to see where their Andersen partners end up, before making a decision. Andersen has also been asking potential buyers to pick up a portion of Andersen's lease obligations, either by signing on for a portion of the lease, or paying another $100,000 to $150,000 to defray the lease liability.

As of June 1, 2002, the other 4 members of accounting's Big Five expected to hire approximately 670 Arthur Andersen LLP partners. *("Who Are Winners at Andersen's Yard Sale?"* Wall St. Journal,, 5/30/02) Deloitte & Touche LLP has signed up about 200 Andersen partners, mostly in the tax specialty in the Chicago, Atlanta, and Dallas regions. Deloitte has also picked up more than 117 former Andersen clients, including Delta Air Lines and United Airlines. Ernst & Young LLP has also signed about 200

Andersen partners, mostly audit experts from the Eastern United States. Ernst has also gained about 150 former Andersen clients, including Federal Express and Oracle. KPMG LLP has also hired approximately 200 Andersen partners, mostly audit, focusing on the West Coast. KPMG has picked up some 133 former Andersen clients, including Household International and Levi Strauss. Finally, PricewaterhouseCoopers plans to hire about 70 Andersen partners, and has gained about 100 former Andersen clients, including Merck Corp. and Freddie Mac. PricewaterhouseCoopers is concerned that picking up any more Andersen partners may bring more liability issues, and could cause integration problems, distractions and morale problems for existing employees. "Having just gone through a significant merger of our own a few years ago (merging with Coopers & Lybrand), we were not prepared to go in that direction," said Dennis Nally, head of U.S. operations for PricewaterhouseCoopers. Furthermore, "Andersen was a very dominant culture, and that does not make for an easy integration."

    The liability that might follow the hiring of a large number of Andersen partners is a major concern as well. The mere fact that corporations have changed accounting firms may not immunize them from SEC investigations. Former Andersen partners may continue to audit the same company from their new firm, and each of the remaining Big Four firms is under at least one SEC investigation. Thus, although business firms are switching auditors, they may end up seeing the government investigators anyway. As one article noted, "the ever-expanding list of corporate accounting scandals is making for strange musical chairs." *Companies Swap Fired Auditors,* Wall St. Journal, July 1, 2002) The Enron-related liability is "still very much unresolved," said Mr. Nally of PricewaterhouseCoopers. The risk for a firm acquiring large numbers of partners is that plaintiffs' lawyers might argue that the firm has acquired a unit of Andersen, with the Enron-related liability that Andersen faces thus transferred with the unit. The other Big Five firms claim that they have consulted with legal counsel and believe they can avoid any liability exposure by hiring individual Andersen partners, rather than acquiring actual offices (units) and by capping the number of Andersen people they hire.

    Second-tier audit firms are also in the market. BDO Seidman LLP directly e-mailed 400 of Andersen's partners on May 10 seeking commitments. The e-mail included a side-by-side comparison of its offer with that of rival Grant Thornton LLP.

Seidman indicates that it has hired some Andersen partners and others will decide in the coming months.

It is not an accounting firm that has hired the largest number of Andersen partners, however. KPMG Consulting, Inc., the company spun off by KPMG LLP last year, has signed an agreement to hire about 550 Andersen consulting partners. KPMG Consulting anticipates bringing on 5,500 to 7,500 Andersen support staff as well. Most of the partner hiring agreements call for about 10 support employees per partner, as requested by Andersen.

So while the venerable firm Arthur Andersen winds down its business, many commentators are wondering what changes in accounting and auditing practices will result from its downfall. The public faith in the accuracy of corporate accounting, auditing and financial disclosure has hit rock bottom, and more and higher standards are being studied by Congress, the SEC, and by the accounting industry. "Within all of the firms, there continues to be the performance of law audits," said former SEC chief accountant Lynn Turner (now a professor). He adds, "Time and again the auditors are missing numbers so big it's literally like driving by Mount Everest and never noticing it." Many reform proposals are circulating in Congress, within the SEC and even President Bush has denounced "corporate wrongdoing," and promised that "no violation of the public trust will be tolerated" in a radio address. Even the accounting industry trade group, the American Institute of Certified Public Accountants, while opposing far-reaching reforms, had agreed that some changes need to be made in corporate accounting and financial disclosure. It will be most interesting to examine how many of the proposed reforms become part of the law in the next year.

LEGAL IMPLICATIONS

The Enron/Arthur Andersen debacles offer business law and legal environment of business instructors almost a textbook example of how many legal principles examined in our classes are fundamentally important to the operations, as well as life and death, of a business firm. Some of the many legal issues highlighted by these scandals are: (1) the law of partnerships, including violation of fiduciary duties and liability of the partnership and individual partners (both civil and criminal); (2) corporate governance, including

such issues as the duties of the officers and directors to the corporation, its shareholders, its employees--both fiduciary and "due care." Also central to the Enron situation is the responsibility of the board of directors to exercise due care in managing the corporation, and the application of the "business judgment rule" is certainly an issue in Enron.
(3) The law concerning pensions and retirement is another key issue, as many Enron employees had most of their 401(k) pension funds invested in Enron stock. For a key period in fall 2001(when the stock price was falling fast) because Enron was changing plan administrators, the employees were prohibited from selling their stock--is that legal? Should the rule be changed? And what are the fiduciary duties of the plan administrators to employees who have most of their savings in company stock, but do not have nearly as much information about the company as the key officials? And how are the pensions of Arthur Andersen partners affected differently, since they are not employees, but owners?

Other important legal issues in the Enron/Andersen case include: (4) Tort law, which is designed to compensate one person who has been economically or physically injured by the "wrongful" acts of another. Accountant's liability for negligence (called malpractice when done by professionals) will be examined through many cases in the coming months. Negligence is the most common tort, and holds one party (perhaps an accountant or auditor or lawyer) liable when that person or firm has rendered a service at a level less than what is expected of a competent professional. There are already numerous tort cases filed against Arthur Andersen by investors, creditors and shareholders of Enron who lost substantial sums due, they say, to the negligence of Arthur Andersen in performing auditing and accounting services. (5) Bankruptcy will be a major legal issue for Enron and perhaps Andersen in the next year. Enron has filed for Chapter 11 bankruptcy, which allows the firm to continue in business while a major "reorganization" of its finances and debts is undertaken. Chapter 11 can be a complex process while the debtor and creditors negotiate on how much of certain debts will be paid, and how and when. In the meantime, the company is totally protected from lawsuits or collection actions outside the bankruptcy court.

(6) Business Ethics is a subject taught as part of many business law and legal environment courses, and there certainly has been no more major scandal in recent years in which a large corporation and its key officers have appeared to violate a wide variety

of ethical principles. The conduct of the officers, directors and key professional advisers of Enron could and should be carefully examined under all major ethical disciplines.

(7) Securities law provides strong sanctions against "insider trading" by company officers and directors who have knowledge of nonpublic material facts (information which would likely affect the stock price if made public). There certainly is a strong argument that the huge sales of Enron stock by Mr. Lay, Mr. Skilling and Mr. Fastow were made at a time they possessed material information about Enron's financial situation which had not been released to the public.

These are only a few of the legal issues involved in the Enron/Andersen case--more will surely appear in the coming months. It should be quite instructive for both students and teachers in "Legal Issues in Business" courses to observe how the principles they are examining in class actually affect business events in the "real world."